“My True Son”

An Anthology of a Journey through Loss

by

Gill Hartley

Foreword by

Fiona Castle

British Library Cataloguing in Publication Data.
A catalogue record for this book is available from the British Library.

ISBN 978 086071 616 7

Cover Picture © Carley Rose Hennigan
Shutterstock

Author's profits and royalties are donated to 'The Compassionate Friends'.

23 Park Road, Ilkeston, Derbyshire DE7 5DA
Tel/Fax: 0115 932 0643 email: info@moorleys.co.uk

Foreword

This poignant collection of poems is borne out of the sad death of Gill's beloved son and only child, Will, at the tender age of twenty-two.

I met Gill for the first time shortly after Will's death. He was a lively, gifted and committed young Christian, in the process of applying to enter the Anglican Church as an ordained minister, when he became unwell.

Gill had already written some very moving poems about him and I realised through reading them the wonderful gift she has of expressing, through poetry, the depths of love she has for the details of life. Before long these poems had grown into an autobiography of her life with Will. You cannot fail to be touched by the creative way Gill describes her memories of her son, such as:

> Before me now lie memories,
> photographs of times remembered
> slip through my hands like paper keys
> unlocking thoughts, releasing words
> and once loved faces flown like birds
> beyond this world…
>
> from her poem, "Keys".

These ways of explaining her love for her son, through the various stages of his life and subsequently through her grief, bring her memories to life. It is said that you have to walk a mile in a person's shoes before you can understand them. You might not have experienced what Gill has gone through but you will better understand the grief of those who have lost children. Some of what she writes is hard to read because of the pain in every line but I hope it will increase people's sensitivity to those facing bereavement of any kind.

Fiona Castle

For Will, my beloved son.

And for all bereaved parents
and their families.

Be Thou My Vision

I visited your grave this morning,
one of the few times I have been there alone.
I don't know why I don't go more often,
maybe because I know you're not there.
Yet, at the same time, I cannot bear to visualise,
you lying there, alone.

It upset me that the grave looked neglected.
Since our last visit, weeds had grown,
I tugged at them, finding them offensive,
But the ground was hard and would not yield.
I wept then,
knelt to hug your headstone,
with its simple inscription,

Will.
1983 – 2006.

I stroked the soft Welsh slate.
It is beautiful.

Around the rim, the words from the hymn you loved,

"You my true Father and I Your true son.
You with me ever and I with You Lord".

(Lord be my vision)
(Book of the Gael)

Introduction

After my son, Will, died at the age of twenty-two, I found myself writing poetry at an extraordinary rate, sometimes as many as three poems a day. When I finally stopped, just over a year later, I had written around one hundred poems, all dedicated to my son.

My son was an extraordinary young man, with an ability to relate to people of all ages. He read history at Birmingham University, gaining a first class honours degree. His chosen subject for his dissertation was Byzantium Iconoclasm – needless to say he was the only student to do this that year! After leaving University, he looked around at possible career choices, none of which held any appeal. In the summer of 2004, we attended New Wine – a Christian conference – together and it was there that Will felt called to enter the Anglican church as an ordained minister. He was in the second stage of his application when he became unwell. The Anglican Church needs young people. Hundreds of people were praying for Will to recover. It just didn't make sense.

But the death of any child does not make sense.

For the first few months after losing Will, I could not stop reading. On a desperate quest to find answers as to why this had happened, I read anything and everything I could lay my hands on concerning loss and the afterlife. But most of the books I read concerning bereavement, involved the loss of a parent or a partner. I would never seek to minimalise such losses but to lose one's child is different. We are programmed to lose our parents one day, perhaps even to lose a partner. We do not expect to outlive our children; it is the wrong order of things. We lose part of ourselves, together with our past, our present and our future.

Shakespeare said, "Give sorrow words". Some of the bereaved parents I have met have told me, "Your poems put into words what others can only feel." If this anthology helps just some bereaved parents on this appallingly lonely journey, then I feel this project has been worthwhile.

You and I were soul mates…

For He has satisfied the thirsty soul and the hungry soul
He has filled with what is good.

Psalm 107:9

Drifting

Do you remember the time
we walked by the Thames
with Luke,
sat side by side on a bench
watching the river drift by?

Our gaze fell on a cricket
that had fallen into the Thames,
it was struggling along in the current,
you turned and caught my eye.
I knew we were both thinking,
how to rescue it from its plight,
when a duck came paddling from nowhere,
and the cricket was gone from our sight.
Although we were sad for the cricket,
we couldn't resist a wry smile.

Such memories as this are so precious
I must treasure every one,
they are all I have to hold on to,
now that you have gone.

Moments

Soothing, to walk down to the wood,
to close the door and leave the hurt behind.
It's not so muddy now, so I can take the path
across the field to where the horses are.
Their soft mouths slough apples from my palm,
their gentle eyes caress my broken heart.
I can feel you standing by my side,
when together we shared moments such as this.
Now I must forever miss
being with you,
sharing moments such as this.

Walking…

When you left every thought
involved walking the dogs with you,
perhaps because of all the years
I'd lived with you at my side.

I still walk with the dog,
but it's not the same without you.
I miss your company,
our conversations,
you sharing your dreams with me.

Kind friends sometimes walk with me now,
but there are still places
where you and I walked,
to which I cannot bear to return.

Some day we'll walk together again,
in a beautiful land where the sun
will not set.

Fleeting

A hoar frost has painted everything white,
Cobwebs hang like white lace,
Intricate.

They had dressed you in a paper gown,
White, with ruffles at your neck and wrists.
Incongruous.

I picture you with your camera,
Capturing the wonder of it all.
Together we will walk,
Revelling in the whiteness.

The church "flower ladies"
Chose white amaryllis.
The simple arrangements flanked your coffin.
Stunning.

Your camera lies unused.
Like mine…

You used to buy me white flowers.
Now,
I buy them for you.
I planted snowdrops at your grave.
Delicate.

I will not take photographs.
Needing no longer
To capture it all for posterity.
But enjoy the beauty while I can.
For it, like you, is…

Fleeting…

Holding hands…

You had such beautiful hands,
so graceful, with your long fingers.
I loved to watch you at work:

Helping in the garden,
tenderly bedding in plants for me.
I loved the way you eased the roots,
gave the plants room to breathe.

Or fashioning wood, the summer you crafted,
so many things for me:
planters and obelisks for my shrubs,
tables and boxes for the birds.

Sitting at the computer with you,
having fun with the internet,
watching your fingers work the keys.
You could type much faster than me.

On the wall at home we have, in a frame,
your handprints from nursery school,
with a printed verse below them:
"… so you can recall,
exactly what my hands looked like,
when I was very small".

When you lay so desperately ill,
I sat beside you holding your hand
and remembered walking with you as a child,
with your trusting hand in mine.

Oh my darling, if only I could hold
those precious hands once more.

Huggles

Lying here, curled up with my tears,
I hug myself, pretending it's you,
imagine your arms around me,
lifting me off my feet.
When you were little,
I'd stand you on the table
together we would dance.
Over the years,
our roles reversed
it was me who stood on the stair.
Through my tears I remember the time,
I first held you in my arms.
all the childhood "huggles" we shared,
the feel of your arms round my neck.

When you lay so desperately ill,
you wanted me to hold you close.
My darling, with all those awful tubes,
it was hard to get near to you.
When I felt your arms around me,
I thought my heart would break.
My child, my arms feel so empty now,
I feel so hollow inside.
knowing I will never again,
be held in your loving embrace.

The things we did together…

In the sweetness of friendship let there be laughter and sharing of pleasures. For in the dew of things the heart finds its morning and is refreshed.

Kahlil Gibran: The Prophet.

Playmates

Sad, you drifted apart.
As children you were inseparable.
I don't know why so many years
intervened.
You chose such different paths,
different schools, new friends.
So many photographs
both families captured
of the two of you, heads together
in sometimes wordless play
and pursuits.
So in tune with one another,
I thought it would last
the two of you
friends for life…

Did you know he was there
the day we buried you?
and wishing you had met
again, maybe in some pub,
somewhere, sometime…

Strange that he should chose to live
in the country you adored.
Perhaps some part of you
has crept into his soul…

Seeds…

Last spring you created a vegetable patch.
I watched you as you turned the earth,
stooping to pick up stones and weeds,
or stopping to smile at me.

We sat together on the compost bags,
entranced by the bold blackbird
sifting out worms by our feet.

That summer we gorged on the fruits of your labour:
runner beans, courgettes and broccoli
and succulent sugar peas.

This spring we looked at the neglected patch,
unable to summon the enthusiasm
to continue with what you'd begun.

Then friends began to give us,
some vegetable plants they had grown
and, from small beginnings,
new life begins to grow.

Scrabble

Sorting through the books,
I find the Scrabble dictionary,
gathering dust,
like the game in its box.

You and I played Scrabble,
we shared a love of words.
We'd try to use up all the letters
and you were the one to keep score.

Words always fascinated you,
the sound and taste of them.
You'd often pause when we read together,
to enjoy and relish a word.

I showed you how to do cryptic crosswords,
you soon became an addict, like me.
Heads together, we'd muse,
searching for answers to clues.

Now my confused mind
reverberates,
With words like "Why?"
and "If".

I will never play Scrabble again,
the game is now unused,
the letters are all in a muddle
and none of the words make sense.

Birds

You and I are in Norfolk,
unaware of the gathering storm
we visit wildlife reserves,
indulging our shared love of birds.

In one of the shops
I buy squirrel proof feeders.
You buy me binoculars,
tell me they are for Christmas,
you want me to have them now…
At home you fill
and hang the feeders
sit, wrapped in your coat,
hoping the birds will come to eat.
But they are wary,
by the time they grow used to them,
everything has changed…

It is spring.
I fill the feeders twice a week.
This year I have bought live mealworms,
a robin, blue tits, great tits
and a nuthatch,
feast on the wriggling fare.

I try to outwit the squirrels,
remembering you chasing them away.
Defeated, I have bought them
their own feeder,
hearing you say, “Oh, Mum!”

Will, are there birds in Heaven,
Or are you watching me with a smile?

Books

You loved books,
as a baby you would sit
studying the print,
I told everyone you were a genius.

Every night
we read to you,
sometimes you'd stop us,
to savour a word,
twirling it round your tongue.

I searched the library
to feed your growing appetite,
now you could read
but still we would share
a bedtime book.

On holiday in Greece,
lying in the shade,
me reading "The Poisonwood Bible",
you reading "Stalingrad".

Now, in your room,
a veritable library,
I study the titles,
knowing that
I will never read them all.
But, like my memories,
I will not part with them.

Driving Through

I am sitting in my car,
thinking of you,
recalling all our travels
together, you and I.

You were my precious passenger,
strapped safely into the car,
in your carrycot
and then in your child seat.

I remember our visits to "Nanny"
before you started school,
you accompanied me everywhere.
You used to call me "Bubby",
we travelled in "Bubby's car."

Setting off on holidays
your impatience to stop for lunch,
or tapping me on the shoulder,
asking, "Bubby, are we there yet?"

All the school years,
beginning with your very first day,
then sharing a car pool with others,
ferrying you to and fro.

When you passed your driving test
our roles began to change,
you became the main driver,
and I your passenger.

During your years at university,
it was always such a delight,
picking you up from Birmingham,
you driving us home.
My little car changed character
with you at the wheel,
it sped along to the rhythm,
of all the CDs you played.

I'm sure my little car misses
you in the driving seat,
now, like me, it must adapt
to life in a slower lane.

New beginnings

You and I,
at our favourite nursery,
you are cramming the car with plants,
tucking them everywhere.
On the way home,
we'll stop to buy more…

The plants were your protégés,
you knew all their Latin names.
I kneel and touch them,
you were green-fingered,
they are thriving…

Such plans, you and I…
here, a pond,
there, some steps,
here, a pergola,
for the roses to climb…

I remember you…
tenderly planting,
watering,
nurturing.

Last summer,
the garden burgeoned.

It will be as we planned.
I will tend your flowers,
learn their Latin names,
nourish them with my tears.

After we took you to see "Cats" your favourite song was "Memories"

Someone said that God gave us memory so that we might have roses in December.

J M Barrie

Keys

Before me now lie memories,
photographs of times remembered
slip through my hands like paper keys
unlocking thoughts, releasing words
and once loved faces flown like birds
beyond this world, or friendships dropped
when mingling of our two worlds stopped.
So many years are captured here
of shared experience, stop the clock;

I'll freeze these smiles and dry the tears.

Album

I'm turning the pages
The first time I held you,
your father, tearful,
you with my mother,
sitting with Geordie
watching cartoons,
I think you thought
all dogs watched TV.

A rear view of you,
sporting a handkerchief hat,
spade in one hand,
bucket in the other,
purposefully heading
towards the sea.

Christmas time:
you unwrapping presents,
sitting on Father Christmas's knee,
gazing in wonder at false beard
and nose,
innocent of the deceit.

The birthday cakes I made,
a sandcastle, a train,
a cricket bat…
You, and your little friends.
I wish I had written the dates
on these pages…

Family parties,
holidays,
the first day at school,
cuddles with me..

On every page…
your radiant smile,
my beautiful silver haired
precious child.

This poem was written when Will was a small child.

Castles in the Air

My eyes caress bent head and flaxen hair,
Your nimble fingers piece together dreams.
I watch you build your castles in the air.

You rummage through the pieces without care,
As a child, life is surely what it seems.
My eyes caress bent head and flaxen hair.

In time you will become aware
That life is not made out of Lego scenes.
I watch you build your castles in the air.

You carefully fit together toy town stair,
For now you can be part of any theme.
My eyes caress bent head and flaxen hair.

In fantasy you move I know not where,
I am no part of your quixotic schemes.
I watch you build your castles in the air.

I wish we could build bridges and repair
Real life with Lego bricks and plastic streams.
My eyes caress bent head and flaxen hair
I watch you build your castles in the air.

Smile, Mum

You always knew how to make me smile,
cheer me up when I felt sad,
with your wonderful sense of humour,
so observant, so perfectly dry.
Even as a child, you made people laugh.
You were the colour in my life.

You were such a talented mimic,
you could adopt anyone's stance,
or their tone of voice, their intonation,
but you were never malicious or unkind.
Being with you was always a joy.
You were the colour in my life.

Just the right remark, at just the right time,
so quick, so clever, so benign.
When something amusing caught your eye,
you'd just look at me and smile.
We were soul mates, you and I.
You were the colour in my life.

I smile when I remember
the bathroom set I bought,
for the house you shared
with your friends at university.
You disappeared upstairs and came down wearing it!
Or the time when Dad brought home from work
the Christmas hamper he'd been given.
You looked like Carmen Miranda
with all that fruit on your head.
Being with you was never dull.
You were the colour in my life.

Oh, my darling, how will I manage,
to survive without you by my side?
Everything seems so grey now.
You were the colour in my life.

Ponds

You introduced me to ponds…
When you were small you began to dig
a hole in the garden.
You were very determined.
Dad began to help.
We lined it,
filled it with water.
We had a pond.

We bought plants to put in it
and around it.
Such excitement when frogs arrived,
then one morning – frogspawn.
I was hooked.
Together we would study the pond,
watch the tadpoles develop,
feed them on Pedigree Chum,
the dogs watching, incredulous.
Our reward: tiny frogs,
thumb nail sized,
perfect.

In our new garden we planned a pond.
You chose the site.
Now we must build it without your help.
But we'll do it for you.

In summers to come,
I'll sit by the pond,
see you bending over it,
calling, "Mummy, come and see!"

I'm still hooked.
But it's not the same.

School Days

I dreaded your first day at school,
I would miss my little companion.
You didn't help by crying
when I walked away.
After a week,
you were happy.
You made new friends.
School was OK.

I longed for half term
and school holidays,
having you with me
all day.

All the school years:
homework,
football,
concerts,
parent's evenings,
exams.

School days over,
you left for university,
This time it was me
who cried.

But not as much,
as I do now.

Snow

The silence
told me it had snowed.
The sky heavy with the promise
of more.
Birds hunched against the whiteness.
I pitied them.

You would have smiled indulgently
to see me,
my coat over my dressing gown,
pyjamas tucked into my boots,
feeding the birds.

I remembered your wonder,
the first time you saw snow,
building your first snowman,
learning to throw snowballs,
crying because the snow burned
your hands.

One half-term it snowed,
we walked the dogs
across the fields,
children were tobogganing on trays, sledges.
One child lent you his sledge,
you launched yourself,
your face shining with delight.
After that, Dad made you a sledge.
By the time it snowed again,
you had outgrown it.

The snow was beautiful today,
but I now see it with different eyes,
it does not enthral as it before,
nothing is as wonderful
as the love we shared.

When the tears fall…

A voice is heard in Ramah, mourning and great weeping. Rachel weeping for her children and refusing to be comforted, because her children are no more.
Jeremiah 31:15

One year on

Even the sky is weeping today,
bleak, salt less tears
drip
from bare branches,
the earth drenched.

Tears trickle down my windows,
stream from my eyes,
blurring my picture
of you…

I close my eyes,
and remember…
I hold your hand,
kiss you,
tell you I love you.
I will see you in the morning…

Bad days…

What do I do on a day like today,
when I find myself in pain?
When I have to pretend everything is all right,
but it isn't,
never will be again.

What do I do when tears keep falling
and I cannot make them stop?
How can I face everyone and smile
when my stomach is tied in a knot?

How can I say it's a "bad day" for me,
and I'm wondering if I can cope?
When no one thinks to ask how I am,
when no one wants to know.

Somehow I'll manage to bluff my way through,
be how I'm expected to be,
conceal my grief until I get home,
then I can break down and weep.

Arrows

They strike without warning,
pierce my heart,
sweep me off my feet,
flatten me.
Force me back
to a time
when tears were fresh,
unchecked.
scalding,
and endless…

I'm with you…
my trembling hands
tracing the loved contours
of your face,
holding your hands,
your fingers cold
against mine.
Kissing you…

Now the tears
are locked away
into the heavy stone
within my heart,
occupying the space
that once was filled
with you…

I welcome these unexpected arrows,
which sometimes take the form,
of careless words,
a time,
a place,
or a sudden memory.

These arrows pierce my armour,
reach the hardened stone
within my heart,
releasing blessed tears
tears that soften
and fill the space
with love and joy
and gratitude for all the years
with you.

Acceptance

This morning I woke
with my heart as heavy
as the grey and leaden sky.
As the tears begin to spill,
I acknowledge that it's true.

Now I understand,
why denial is a gift from God,
my child, how could I possibly believe,
that I really have lost you?

How could I accept,
I will never see you again?
Never hold you in my arms,
you will never be coming home.

Now sadness is displacing,
the cushion of denial,
the truth is destroying me,
my pain is deeper still.

Tears

Can this sound be coming from me?
primitive wailing,
heart-rending cries,
tears, tears,
endless tears.
Dear God, will this well of grief
ever run dry?
Feelings of emptiness,
depths of despair,
huge and overwhelming loss.
Dear God, I am chopped in two,
since my only child returned to you.

Now

Please don't ask me to do anything,
I just want to lie here and cry,
every day is a mountain to climb,
all I really want is to die.

I have been making such an effort,
to do what I'm expected to do,
smile and face the world,
when I just want to be with you.

I'm caught in this painful present,
it is all my grief will allow,
I can't look to the past
or the future,
every waking moment is now.

All that I can manage
is one sorrowful step at a time,
no one can really help me,
this grief is exclusively mine.

I just long for the day, my darling,
when I will see you again,
until then I will try to exist
and live with this lonely pain.

Please show me that you are happy
and not grieving the way I do,
this knowledge would bring some comfort,
until I can be with you.

So do not worry about me,
just leave me alone with my tears,
I'll be all right, I'll manage somehow,
to survive the coming years.

Times of anger and frustration…

Every man is a master of grief except he that has it.

Shakespeare: Much ado about nothing. Act 3, Scene 2

Moving On

My friend, I know you don't mean to hurt,
when you tell me I will "move on".
That "Time will heal, you will feel better",
my friend, we've just buried my son.
My friend, I watched my only child die,
the precious child I had borne.
The child I'd adored for twenty-two years,
the child who'd become a young man.
My soul mate and my closest friend,
quite simply the joy of my life.
When he died, my future died too.
He had shared his dreams with me,
the wife he prayed he would meet,
the children he prayed they would share.
He talked of his Lord, in whose church he would serve,
a future we will never see,
So my friend, please don't tell me,
how you think I should be.

Clichés

"I'm sorry to hear of your loss,
I know exactly how you feel,
I can remember how I felt,
when I lost my cat."

==========

"You must try and put it behind you."
"Get on with your life."
"Move on."

That's fine, but please could you tell me,
Where I'm supposed to move to?

Second Time Around

We should be “feeling better”,
after all, it all happened last year.
We’re expected to be “over it now?”
and pack you away with our tears.

What could be further from the truth?
Last year seems a blur somehow.
I can’t remember all we said and did,
all I can think of is... *now.*

Now your room is still empty,
your shelves are still full of your books,
your clothes still hang in your cupboards,
your dressing gown hangs from its hook.

Now you no longer call me,
I don’t hear your voice saying, “Mum!”
I cannot hold you or see you,
my grieving has barely begun.

It hurt, the second birthday,
without your presence here,
now you would be twenty-four
we missed your twenty-third year.

You didn’t send us birthday cards,
or send me flowers this year,
on Mothering Sunday I cried all day,
but still you did not appear.

The truth is we’ll never recover,
time will not heal our wounds,
our pain will linger with each passing year,
and anniversaries come too soon.

Life goes on…

Why must people brush aside
my grief, with the words,
"Life goes on."
I want the world to stop,
how can it exist without you?

Can't they see my life has shattered,
every step like walking on glass,
every breath an effort,
every thought is of you.

I feel I am an actress,
on stage with a part to play,
the words I utter are not mine,
I'm not the person you see.

The pattern of every day life,
is fragmented, no longer real,
every thing is trivial now,
I view the world through tears.

Yes, life does go on,
the world is unaware
it's been robbed of one of its treasures,
it's a poorer world without you.

More Clichés

"Are you feeling better now?"
Someone asked me the other day.
"Ask me in twenty years," I said.

"Oh, that's good." she replied.

And loneliness…

At the innermost centre of all loneliness is a deep and powerful yearning for union with one's lost self.

Brendon Francis

Drowning

Why are some days worse than others?
Yesterday, I coped quite well,
I walked the dog, met a friend for lunch,
passed the day with very few tears.
But today my world is a tear filled ocean
I have stumbled through,
not knowing whom I can speak to,
just longing for someone to care.
Too deep in my grief to pick up the phone,
afraid if I do, no one will be there.

No One Came

No one called, no-one came,
just like yesterday, just the same.
Endless minutes, rolled into one,
"Over my grief?" I've barely begun.
to accept the truth that you have gone.

The time crawls by,
drip feeding the knowledge
that I watched you die.
Truth so appalling, that still I deny
and echo the question,
"Why, God, Why?"

Keeping busy

In the mornings I walk Luke.
He chases squirrels,
sniffs and socialises
He is such a busybody.
his busyness keeps me occupied.
just for an hour – or two.

Back home, I turn the computer on,
busy myself writing,
answering emails,
trying to sort the muddle I'm in.
This keeps me busy,
for an hour - or two.

In the afternoons,
it's hard to keep busy,
that's when fatigue creeps in,
I try to ignore it –
must keep busy,
not give myself time to think.
I tire myself out, fidget,
make tea and try to sit still
and watch the busy bumblebees,
bumbling around…
like me.

Evening time,
while your father cooks supper,
I might be busy writing to you,
or writing a poem, checking emails,
and, now that summer is here,
after supper I can work in the garden,
there's lots to do out there,
I water and prune,
keep very busy,
until darkness drives me indoors.

And now it's night time
and all I can do
is lie on my bed…

and weep.

Moonscape

I'm adrift in this new country,
I did not ask to come here.
I imagine the moon must be like this:
emptiness everywhere,
rain coloured stones
and faceless rocks,
splintered earth
that hurts my feet.
There is no horizon,
in this landscape belonging to Grief.

I can't find this road they told me about,
for this journey I am having to make.
That's strange because I understand
countless others have been here before.
But I've searched this barren landscape,
I can't see another soul,
there don't seem to be any signposts,
I have never felt so alone.

I read that Grief can isolate one,
make us feel misunderstood,
no one can really understand
exactly what we feel.
I realise there is no prequel
for those who walk with grief.

But I must make a friend of Grief,
if I am to survive,
only he can accompany me,
on this chapter in my life.
Grief provides the buffer
between us and our enemy, Death.
We are allowed to wander,
at will in this lonely place,
until at last there comes a time
when we stumble into Peace.

Muddled

I'm told grief is a process,
with stages
through which I should move,
then I will mourn successfully,
not make a mess of my grief.

But grief is a messy business,
I can't see a pattern to this.
I am in a whirlpool
I don't where I should be.
One minute I feel anger,
the next I'm in despair,
or lost in utter confusion,
trying to bargain with God.
Sometimes the pain
is too much to bear,
at other times I feel nothing
and think maybe I've died too.

I wonder who sets these patterns,
telling us how we should be,
when we find ourselves
in quicksand,
in the depths of the sea.
When the waves engulf us,
dragging us to and fro,
we cannot hold fast to the guidelines,
that tell us which way we should go.

Paper Thin

I'm becoming quite adept
at pretending that I'm fine.
I'm doing very well,
I'll be OK, given time.
I talk about my faith in God
say that I'm holding on,
and I believe that, one day,
I'll be in Heaven with my son.

I talk of all the things I'll do
to make him proud of me,
I say how pleased he'd be to know
I'm writing this poetry.

I say how in the future,
God will use my pain
to help others with their grief,
my suffering will not be in vain.

I've become quite adept at donning,
this facade for others to see,
I tell myself I'm protecting them,
from having to face the real me.

But beneath this bravado,
behind this mask I wear,
lies a heart that is broken,
a mother, drowning in tears.

Eternity

My darling son,
I do not know
how I can live
without you.

Despite my belief
that you are in Heaven,
and when God calls me home,
I will see you again.

It is the here and now
I'm afraid of,
knowing I must spend
the rest of my days,
here,
now,

without you.

Sometimes I reflect…

It is admirable how many millions of people come into and go out of the world, ignorant of themselves and the world they live in.

William Penn

Mothering Sunday

I am sitting here,
holding the beautiful card
you made for me …

two years ago, today.

I have twenty-one such cards from you,
and treasure every one.
From the first card,
bought by your father,
and scribbled on, by you.
to the card I am holding now.

As my tears fall,
I reflect,
maybe we have got it wrong
as mothers we should give our children the cards,
for teaching us the meaning
of love.

My darling *Will,*
I'll try to dry my tears,
and dedicate this special day,
my precious son…

to you.

Ticking…

Your watch still lies on your desk,
where you left it that morning.
Today, I picked it up,
it had stopped…

You were not good with watches,
one you lost at school,
another, on the beach.

This one you looked after.
Silver, with a blue face.
A clever watch,
it would set the hour automatically
when the clocks changed.
Linked to some computer,
you said.

You would set this watch
to time the talks you were preparing.
Or use it as an alarm,
to waken you.

It hurts to find your watch
has stopped.

Like you.

Love has a price…

C.S. Lewis said:
"Grief is the price we pay for love"
many others have said that, too.
If this be true, then I will give
the rest of my life
to pay the cost of loving,
and being loved by,
you.

For the love we shared is priceless
and my grief too small a cost,
to pay for all those precious years
and recompense my loss.

Gloves…

For Mum and Will

You hung your coat
on the bedroom door,
that last time
you came to stay.

In the pocket were your gloves.

The coat hung there
until we sold the house,
then, I had to take it down.
I gave it away.

But I kept your gloves.

For years now,
I have kept your gloves
in my dressing table drawer.
Sometimes, I lift them out,
hold them in my hands,
remembering yours…

Now, I have another pair of gloves
to keep with yours.

Your grandson's hands
were the same shape as mine.
Sometimes he and I would press our hands
together, and smile.

Now these gloves too,
retain the shape and feel
of hands I loved
and are no more.

Now,
when I hold your gloves,
I hold his, too…

and remember.
the three of us,

Hand in hand.

Family Ties

Will, I wonder, have you met
the grandfather you never knew?
Were you drawn to one another
by a bond you both could sense?

Is he reunited with the wife he so loved?
The grandmother you knew as "Nanny"
whom you adored and lost.

Did he know of the grandchildren
born after he had died?
And that he now has great grand children too?

I know you shared a name
and perhaps his curly hair.
But have you discovered
his love of carving wood?
A legacy that his own father
passed down the line to you?

My darling, I pray you understand him
in the way I never could.
And get to know the man
I never really knew.

And when we are together again
and I hold you in my arms,
I pray that for the first time
I will get to hug my father too.

The Yellow Wood

A tribute to the Road not Taken, by Robert Frost.

This morning I walked through a yellow wood,
there was wind and rain last night
but the leaves had held fast
to the trees,
reluctant to shed their glorious
autumn colours
too soon.

This year,
autumn has been beautiful,
the low sun highlighting its rich display.
For the first time since you left,
I wanted to capture it
and thought of your camera,
unused, collecting dust.

Once, when you were small,
we walked in the same wood,
reached a spot where four paths crossed.
We differed as to which path
would lead us back to the car.
You wept, knowing you were right,
I had to relent, and yes,
you were.

You always had a sense of direction
knowing which path you should take.
With you at my side I felt safe.
Now, I cannot follow you,
the path you have taken
leads away from me
and is blurred by tears
and fallen leaves…

The River

We've been caught in a river,
swept along by its pace.
hopelessly clutching at driftwood
something to make us feel safe.

Violent storms
lashed the river
causing the waves to surge,
plunging us into depths
of darkness and despair.
filling our mouths with grit,
leaving us gasping for air.

Sometimes the waters were still.
Deceived by the calm,
we were lulled in to hoping
you would escape unharmed.

But then, that dreadful night,
the river cast us ashore
onto land that was cruel and jagged,
a land where our hopes were scorned.

One day we'll return to the river,
hopefully follow its course.
Trusting we will find you,
when the river reaches its source.

The Moat

There is a cold grey moat,
between me and the rest of the world
And I have lifted the drawbridge,
so I cannot be disturbed.

No one but God can understand,
the deep, deep pain I face,
so I must spend this time alone,
the darkness I will embrace.

I cannot chase after the sun,
there is only one route I can take,
I must travel through the darkness,
then I might find God's grace.
For somewhere in the shadows,
there must be a glimmer of light,
something to reassure me,
you are safe in the arms of Christ.

And though I am lost without you,
I know that somehow God is still there
and he will guide me through the darkness
and rescue me from despair.

Rainbow's End...

I am listening to Desert Island Discs.
The guest makes her first choice:
Somewhere, over the Rainbow
from the *Wizard of Oz.*

I too have a choice:
I can turn the radio off,
and with it, my pain.
Or I can listen,
let the pain wash over me
allow the tears to flow...

> I am lying in the bath,
> in the bathroom of our first home.
> Across the landing,
> in the small nursery,
> your father is soothing you to sleep.
>
> I imagine him stroking your head,
> which you loved us to do,
> and playing the little wind-up musical box,
> over and over again.
> I can hear the soft notes,
> unfolding the theme,
> *Somewhere, over the Rainbow...*

On the radio,
the beautiful voice sings;
Somewhere, over the Rainbow
Way up high,
There's a land that I heard of
Once, in a lullaby.

My darling, if only I could
fly over that rainbow,
and wake up, as the song says,
where the clouds are far behind me...
and find you.

Instead I will search
for the rainbow's end...

And you.

And I dream…

Take if you must, this little bag of dreams.
Unlock the cord and they will wrap you round.

Yeats

Dreaming…

Will, was it you?
Was it you who consoled me,
when I woke weeping from my dream?
Was it your voice saying,
"It's all right. I love you."

I dreamed you returned,
a child again,
I was so happy to see you,
to hold you in my arms.

But as I held you and asked,
"Darling, did you know you died?"
I began to awaken from my dream
and knew that nothing had changed.

I was crying,
re-entering my world of pain,
then I heard a voice:
"It's all right. I love you."

Will, was it you?
Or was it God
reassuring me,
that you are safe
and He still loves me?

Echoes

You are sitting outside in the car,
it is dark, very dark.
I find you, ask,
"*Will*, do you have a torch?"
You get out
and show me the way.

As we walk, you are talking,
laughing.
I do not reply.
No, I must listen…
to your voice
and your laughter…

I must remember

the sound of you…

Journeying on…

We are travelling together,
as so often in the past.
Some outing, we have Luke with us.
a bus is waiting…
people are boarding, all with dogs,
Border collies, like Luke.

I board ahead of you,
leave you to park the car.
The bus is full,
I climb to the upper deck,
find us a seat.

You do not come.
Anxious,
I ask someone to look after Luke,
get off the bus,
begin to scan the crowds,
then, I realise…

Relating this to a friend,
he observed:
"The bus was not going anywhere…"

No, but it will…

And I must journey on….

The seasons change...

It was the season of Light, it was the season of Darkness, it was the spring of hope, it was the winter of despair.

Charles Dickens
A Tale of Two Cities

Marking time…

Wherever I am at this moment,
it's the only place I can be,
I will dwell in this darkness,
holding you close,
and pray to God
to comfort me.

There was a time…

when the sun always shone,
the sky an endless vivid blue.

There was a time…
when the birds sang night and day,
when the colour of flowers
was intense.
The grass unbelievably green.

There was a time…
when everyone smiled,
when happiness was not just a word.

There was a time…
when memories did not hurt
but made us smile.
There was a time,
when we looked to a future,
bright
with dreams for you.

There was a time…

When you were alive…

And so was I.

Changing scenes

We decided to redecorate your room
knowing, had you been here,
it would have been done
by now.

You chose the curtain fabric.

I matched the colours
for the walls and carpet.
Wondering if you would approve.

To decorate
we had to move your belongings
from your room…
your books,
posters,
photographs,
computer,
your bedside table,
all the odds and ends.
And your bed.

In the drawer under your bed…
Baby clothes,
your first shoes,
old school ties,
your cub shirt and scarf…

The room finished,
we put everything back,
tried to make it look as it did before.
It looks nice.

But something is missing…

Spring

Spring arrived too early this year.
The mild winter has fooled the trees,
already, they are in bud.
Bulbs are pushing through,
snowdrops kiss the earth.

Now the cold weather has arrived,
Yesterday it snowed.
Perhaps the spring will realise,
it cannot be spring
without you.

The trees are confused,
the winter has been too short,
they have not had time to rest.
Like me
they must find the strength,
to see the summer through.

Today, the sun shone,
despite the bitter cold,
it warmed the earth,
melted away the snow.
Perhaps the sun's rays
will rescue the trees,

and me.

Autumn

With the dark evenings
come memories,
memories that make us weep.
A long hot summer,
passed
without you.

Last autumn, your life
began to fall apart,
your strength to ebb away.

Now the trees are turning again,
shedding leaves,
like tears.

It seems as if my life has been frozen
just waiting for you
to come home.
Perhaps, when the evenings lighten
and spring comes…

but I know that you will not return.

I will not see you again,

until my winter is here…

Christmas tree

Stored, in our loft,
a Christmas tree.
It isn't real.
You preferred artificial
not liking the thought
of all those young trees,
felled.

It was the same every year…
reaching into the loft,
bringing down the boxes marked
"Christmas".
fitting the tree together,
straightening its branches.

Decorating it.

Trinkets for the tree
collected over the years.
Some you had made when you were small.
And every year
the same hunt for spare bulbs,
for lights that failed to work,
but did, eventually.

It was the same every year,
until that Christmas…

Cabaret

The first day of Christmas…

Christmas Eve…
Limp from weeping,
I gaze out of the window,
see, through my tears: a glint of gold.
I throw a chicken leg onto the lawn,
call your father, who arrives just in time
to see the red kite swoop.
Magnificent.

The stunning spectacle lifts my mood,
but the cabaret is not finished…
a posse of red-legged partridge arrive.
I count them …one, two, three…
twelve RLP's! (we christened them thus,
thinking how much they resembled OAPs.,
always in pairs, clucking away).

The finishing touch…
a green woodpecker on the neighbour's grass.

Will, how kind of God to allow you
to arrange all this,
a Christmas present for your mum,
to make me smile.

Wrapping up…

All those years,
buying presents for you…
Collecting,
wrapping,
hiding.

Christmas mornings,
you awake at dawn,
and us,
yawning, sipping tea,
watching you unwrap your gifts.
Enjoying your delight.

* * * * * * * * * * * * * * *

I have been wrapping presents,
taking care
my tears won't smudge
the messages on the gifts,
for my sister's grandchildren…

I will never wrap presents for mine…

I just miss you…

Sometimes, only one person is missing, and the whole world seems depopulated.

Alphonse de Lamartine

Silence

The house echoes with the silence.
No music expanding the walls
of your room.

You laughing at the "Simpsons"
or shouting at the computer.
Your phone calls,
your conversation.

You calling, "Mum!"
Playing with the dog.
The sound of the fridge door opening –
you were always hungry.

You revving the car.
The CD's you played when driving.
Your footsteps.
Your key in the door.

I miss the sound of you.

All senses of you…

Missing you

A new day has begun,
another day of missing you,
knowing your room is empty,
I can't go in and wake you –
see you smiling at me.
We can't breakfast together,
or take the dog to the woods,
another day without you,
I breakfast with my tears.

The day drags on
without your presence,
you saying "I love you, Mum."
You cannot go shopping with me,
sit down and share some lunch.
You are not here to make me laugh,
or to have a row.
I realise this is forever,
I lunch alone with my tears.

I miss you so much in the evenings,
when the darkness encloses me,
there's an empty chair at the table,
set for two instead of three.
I will never again prepare you a meal,
or enjoy something you've cooked,
watch a favourite programme with you,
or discuss the events of the day,
tell you to turn the computer off,
not to stay up too late.

I dread the sleepless night to come,
when my pillow is damp with my tears
and tomorrow will bring more heartache
and my tears will measure the years.

Too Long

All this time I've been thinking,
you cannot be dead,
it's not real.

But this has gone on much too long,
this isn't a joke,
it's real.

You see, it's nearly six months,
since that dreadful night
and all this time I've been thinking,
if I went back to your hospital room
it would all be all right…
you'd be there.

But your room at home feels empty,
it's seven months since you slept here.
it is still just as you left it,
your watch and wallet lie on your desk,
your jacket hangs from the chair.

It's time you stopped playing this game now.
it's time you came back home.
but deep inside, I know you cannot,
this isn't a joke,

it's real.

Cloudless

Now the clouds are moving away
I stand exposed to the glare
of the sun, it burns relentlessly.
I am stripped bare of all pretence.
My pain is exposed
for all to see.

Now the clouds are drifting away,
the sun's rays focus on me,
I cannot escape,
there's no place to run
from the blinding truth
that you have gone.

Now the clouds are drifting away
It's you I miss,
not the memories
or the things that we did,
it's you.

Now the clouds are moving away
It's you that I can see:
Your smile,
Your eyes,
Your voice,
Your warmth,
Your touch,
Your hands,
Your walk,
Your laugh,
You.

Now the clouds have moved away,
it's you
I miss.

You.

Closed doors

Your room is my refuge,
here, with you,
I write…

I keep the door closed,
lest cooking smells,
or curious eyes,
dilute the presence
of you.

In this room
cupboards contain
your clothes,
camping equipment,
camera and tripod,
boxes and files,
my denial and pain.
These doors are closed
even to me.
I must hold on to these contents,
this tangible evidence
of you.
Because if not,
my darling,
should you return,
how could I explain?

Timeless

I watch your face and hold your hand in mine,
Talk to you of love and all that we have been.
So much to say and now there is no time.

I could pretend that everything is fine,
That sitting here with you is but a dream.
I watch your face and hold your hand in mine.

My life with you has been sublime,
Just as I knew that it would be.
So much to say and now there is no time.

This must be part of some design,
For things are never as they seem.
I watch your face and hold your hand in mine.

Your wondrous eyes have lost their loving shine,
You no longer play a part in this sad scene.
So much to say and now there is no time.

My son, I wish we could rewind
The clock and start with a new theme.
I watch your face and hold your hand in mine
So much to say and now there is no time.

Being Here

I am sitting in your room
surrounded by you…

I feel like an intruder,
entering, without knocking
on your door.
All your private thoughts
are here…
and your books, your writing,
the photographs you took,
your posters, your music.
Your slippers by your bed.
Your bed… yes especially…
your bed…
and your scent, the scent
that only I, your mother,
would know.

I switch on your computer,
it opens onto your life
so many files…
"My documents. My pictures,
My testament.
My life…"

Everything that is you,
my precious son,
is here.

But not you.
Not you.

Identity

Once I had a role,
I was a mother.
Now you have gone,
I am childless.

I no longer know who I am.

There was a time when I thought,
you justified my existence.
You would achieve so much,
I would live my life,
through you…

Now,
in my mirror…
a new reflection.

You taught me so much,
by dying, even more…
opening my eyes
to a suffering world.
My values have totally changed.

You gave me so much,
now I must put something back.
Use the precious gift you left me…
love.

I ask "Why?"

If the Lord is with us, why has all this happened to us?
Judges 6: 13

Revolving

My dearest son,
you lie so still,
no warmth, no touch,
no answering smile.
My precious child,
this is not how it should be
that you should die
ahead of me.

How could our God,
our God of love,
permit such suffering,
such a terrible loss?

Lord, my son had given his life to you,
achieved so much
so much to do.
Why did you allow my son to die?

Yet, despite my grief,
my confusion and pain,
I must hold on,
must still believe.

When you asked your disciples,
"Will you leave me too?"
In his confusion, St Peter replied,
"Lord Jesus, to whom can we turn,
but you?"

Lord Jesus, to whom can **I** turn,
but You?

Jigsaw

I'm trying to do this jigsaw,
but I don't know where to begin,
some of the pieces are missing,
and none of them seem to fit in.

I can't even find the picture
of what it's supposed to be,
some pieces seem completely blank,
there's no pattern I can see.

I cannot make any sense of it,
I do not understand,
each piece should fit in somewhere,
there must be some kind of plan.

Perhaps if I try harder,
I'll find some pieces that are straight,
if I can fit them together,
then something may resonate.

Maybe it doesn't matter too much,
if some pieces have gone astray,
as long as I have some idea,
what the picture is meant to say.

You were so clever at jigsaws,
even when you were small,
you seemed to know instinctively
which piece you were looking for.

Perhaps if I close my eyes,
and pretend you are here with me,
we can finish the jigsaw together
and see what the picture will be.

Why…?

Jesus, why did you allow
my son to be taken from me?
Why did you allow the enemy
this small victory?
Jesus, I so want to believe
Your battle against Death is won,
but how can this be a comfort
to me here, without my son?

I'll never know
what he might have accomplished
if he'd remained longer on earth,
he wanted so much to serve You,
tell others of his faith.
You bestowed on him
so many gifts to pass on,
why did You give him so much,
then allow him to die so young?

Jesus, there is a need in Your church
for young men such as my son,
he could have achieved so much for You,
his service had barely begun.
How can we possibly understand
Your purpose in letting him die?
To us, with our limited knowledge,
we can only ask You, "Why?"

But, despite my confusion
my suffering and my pain,
I choose to believe my son is safe,
I choose to hold on to my faith.
Jesus, I know You told us
Your ways are not ours,
so, despite my uncertainty,
I will still stand on Your word
and long for the day when You return
to reclaim Your World.

Are You there, Jesus?

Are You there, Jesus,
do You hear my cries,
do You hear me weeping,
long into the night?

Do You understand, Lord,
how much I miss my son,
my life has lost its meaning,
now that he has gone?

I know I should believe,
that he is safe with You,
but that is where I struggle
and wonder if it's true.

I have no way of knowing,
if You are there for me
I cannot feel Your presence,
in my agony.

I so long for You to help me,
some knowledge that You care,
that, despite all my doubts and fears,
You are really there.

Please answer when I cry to You,
let me know my son is safe,
please give me some comfort,
forgive my lack of faith.

For I am weak and You are strong,
and only You can bring,
the peace of mind I long for,
the courage to go on.

Be Still…

Lord, my heart has been broken
as only a mother's can be,
help me believe my son's happier with You,
than here, on earth, with me.
Jesus, I miss my son,
I miss the life I once knew,
but I also miss having You in my life,
please help me turn back to You.

Lord, please guide my hand to write
words of love to You.
Loosen my tongue that I might sing
songs of praise to You.
Here, in this place of peace and love,
may all suffering souls reside
in Your loving arms,
let go of our pain,
be still…
and remember
it was for us

You died…

Written on retreat
at St Mary's Convent, Wantage.

I have regrets…

God, give us grace to accept with serenity the things that cannot be changed, courage to change the things that should be changed and the wisdom to distinguish the one from the other.

Reinhold Niebuhr

Yearning…

My darling, I yearn…
to hear your voice, your laughter.
You ringing me, saying, “Hi, Mum”

You telling me your news,
your hopes and plans.
I even miss our arguments,
but regret the times I said,
“It’s not what you say,
it’s the tone in your voice…”
Now, I would give my life
to hear that tone again.

I miss our midnight chats.
Climbing in beside you in the morning,
just to talk.

I remember your singing,
you telling me how a tune went,
You always said, “dee dee dee”
not “la la la”

I remember the first time I heard your cry,
our joy to hear your first giggle.
You used to call me “Bubby”
you couldn’t say your “Ms”
when you were small.

But most of all, my darling son,
I miss you saying,

“I love you, Mum”

I yearn…

Missing out…

All your hopes
and dreams,
such plans…
such dreams…

I will never
see you fall in love,
dance with you at your wedding,
cradle your children
in my arms.

Your friends have lost
the kindest friend they will ever know,
when they marry,
you will not be there.
never be a "best man"
or lead your daughter up the aisle.

I'm in your room,
surrounded by
your hopes…
your dreams…
posters of places
you were planning to visit,
books you'd yet to read.

My sister's grandchildren
loved you,
but they are young
and may not remember.

Such happiness
when you heard God's call,
how could we have known,
He was actually calling you home?

Shells

When I summon the courage
to drive again,
I find, in the car,
your water bottle,
your jacket and scarf.

And shells and pebbles
from our last holiday.

I pick up one of the shells,
some sand falls…

all those holidays…
and you and I
searching for shells
or pebbles of unusual shapes.
Once we filled a matchbox
with perfect miniature shells.

At home, in your room,
all those treasures
gather dust on the windowsill.

Except for one…

That last time,
buffeted by the east wind,
we watched a lone seal
swimming in the chilling North sea.
It was so cold.
I wish I had realised
what a struggle it was for you.

Then, you saw the pebble,
stooped to pick it up
and silently gave it to me.

That tiny heart-shaped white pebble,
is so very precious now.
Tears fall and I'm back,
walking on that beach
with you.

Technically Challenged

You were fond of telling me
how I am "technically challenged".
You were the technology expert,
always on hand to help.
Now I sit bewildered
by all this computer stuff,
trying to recall the things you taught me,
I realise now I didn't listen enough.

Some of the things I remember,
and there are some things I can do,
like turning on the computer,
even sending an Email or two.
I've even managed to open a file
to write this book for you.

But when I encounter problems,
I'm lost without you here.
The margins are all in a muddle
and all these odd icons appear…
I have a winking and smiling paperclip man
and I cannot get rid of him,
all these unwanted symbols
seem to appear on a whim.

But are things you would be proud of,
that I have managed to achieve,
I had a "talk" with your friend Ed,
via Messenger, would you believe?
Although that was a happy mistake,
not something I'd set out to do.
And at last I can send text messages,
now it's too late to text you…

I know I still have so much to learn
I may get there eventually,
But darling, I so wish I could tell you
some of the things I have done,
yet somehow I know you are by my side,
silently cheering me on.

When the singing stopped…

When we were young
my mother always sang.
I loved to hear her in the mornings,
singing along
to Housewives' Choice.
My sister claims it embarrassed her,
when her friends asked,
"Is that your mother singing?"
when she walked with them past our house.
My mother sang until my father died,
and then she didn't sing anymore.

My parents thought I could sing,
and sent me have my voice trained,
Madame Bosck,
the singing teacher,
said I had the pitch and the power.
Then I left my music on the bus,
and I didn't have lessons anymore.

But I always sang in the bath,
a safe place
and the acoustics were good.
I sang in the bath until I was married,
when my husband put his head round the door,
and uttered the words he regrets to this day,
"Are you in pain, my dear?"
It was only meant as a joke,
I know,
but I didn't sing in the bath anymore,
until my son was born,
what joy,
to sing nursery rhymes with him.

As he grew older,
we still sang together,
often driving along in the car.
Then my son died,
and the world stopped singing,
and now I don't sing anymore.

But we have hope…

He will wipe every tear from their eyes. There will be no more death or crying or pain, for the old order of things has passed away. He who was seated on the throne said, "I am making everything new!"

Revelation 21

Fear

When you were a baby,
tucked safely in your cot,
I would creep into your room,
check you were still alive.

Time passed,
I began to hope,
but the fear
became part of my life.

You grew into adulthood,
I began to relax,
maybe my fears were unfounded,
you would always be part of my life.
When you gave your life to God,
I thought at last you were safe.

But God does not protect us
from life in this fallen world.
He warned us we would suffer,
yet not to be afraid.

I must find the strength
to carry on without you
and pray until we meet again,
you are safe in the arms of God.

Will Silver

These lovely trees reflect so much of you,
Your slender grace,
Your sparkling silver hair.
When the breeze rustles the leaves
In summer.
We'll hear you whisper,
"Do not weep, for I am always near."
And those of us who knew and loved you,
Will hear your laughter and see you smiling
Through our tears.
And all you gave us of your love and friendship
Will endure until we meet with you once more.

16th October 2006
Written for Will's tree planting on 29th October 2006

Hope

Like me, the garden is desolate,
the mantle of winter has cast us both down.
Seed heads have replaced the flowers,
the rose arch is a bower of thorns.
The hammock where we swung on sunlit evenings,
stands dormant in the dank, anaemic air.
Everything looks so abandoned,
bleak and starved of light.
The garden, like me, is bereaved,
now summer has turned into night.

This morning, I searched the sleeping garden,
trod the sodden, yellowed grass,
knelt amongst the hibernating bushes,
cast aside the crumbling leaves,

and then I found
a thrusting shoot of crocus.

Happiness

My darling son,
I always thought
the day I gave birth to you
was the happiest of my life.

Now I realise,
that was true
of every moment spent with you

But the best has yet to come:

the truly happiest day will be
when I'm reunited with you.

****

My True Son…

Will, do you know of the poems I have written?
Do you read them, every one?
Do you approve of the title of this book?
I know you loved to think
that you are one of His sons.

He shared you with me for twenty–two years,
And I do not think He will mind,
if I call you,

***My** True Son.*

Acknowledgments

Heartfelt thanks to my friend and writing tutor, Jan, who read every poem I wrote, made suggestions, encouraged me, and without whose love and support I would never have brought this anthology to completion.

To Graham Hartnell and Joyce and Malcolm Wiles for help with computer problems and the graphics. I am, as my son was always telling me, technically challenged!

To Diane Brazier, for her help and inspiration with the illustrations.

To Fiona Castle for writing the foreword.

My husband, Edwin, for his patience and support in the face of his own pain and to The Compassionate Friends, who gave us a lifeline.

And finally to Moorley's for their faith in me.

'The Compassionate Friends'
Help and support for bereaved parents and their families.
TCF National Office: 53 North Street, Bristol BS3 1EN
Tel: 0845 120 3785 Helpline 0845 123 2304
www.tcf.org.uk info@tcf.org.uk

The Child Bereavement Charity
Tel: 01494 446648
www.childbereavement.org.uk
Resources and support for bereaved families and children.

Author's profits and royalties are donated to 'The Compassionate Friends'.